A Near Life Experience

Namir Stephan

To Elena and Catrina

Preface

The story of this poem began with my love for nature and our beautiful earth.

On a warm September day, after long hours at work I decided to go for a walk in the woods. Arriving there, I was greeted by tall Maple and Pine trees generously lining and shading the narrow trail. They freely breathed in what I breathed out at the end of a working day. As I moved through this calm and secluded yet vibrantly living world, I could hear, from a distance, the waters of the Clinton River murmur to the rocks. The urge to sit still and admire the shallow waters flowing gracefully gently came upon me. I clearly recognized that pebbles on the riverbed were sitting in peace, gazing at the water plants doing their hula with the ebb and flow of the exuberant river waters.

In my eyes, this hidden spot in the midst of nowhere was no less glamorous than the Grand Canyon or Yosemite. Here, I could see nature as so full of wonder. This sense was mystifying, as it carried me back in time, on a journey to think about God, knowing how long this river has preceded me! There was this gentle and tender breeze conveying a feeling of longing, or maybe a feeling of belonging to Earth and all it has birthed. Two words rhymed in my head: *mystery* and *history*, and in that moment something unforeseen happened, something that I couldn't fathom or even describe at the time; it felt as if a mighty gate opened and spontaneously rushing out came the *words*, *expressions* and *images*. But, with great hesitation, I reached for my phone to type in few words. Then, as baffled as I was, I quickly realized that what I had written sounded like poetry, and in fact, was poetry. A bigger realization followed. That these previously distinct but now simultaneous experiences are one and the same. All nature and poetry and everything else are from the same Breath.

Perplexed and overcome with self-doubt, and for good reason, I tucked my phone back into my pocket. "Of course this couldn't be," I thought to myself. I am not capable of crafting such words, such ideas, such poetry. I am not a poet nor was I ever interested in poetry. And so, never having read poetry, unaware of its meaning or course, I felt so strongly that I could not be a poet, let alone write poetry. My inexperience coupled with the simple fact that English is my third language defining my humble vocabulary would make such a task impossible so why should I bother? But why do I have this young poetic inclination? I kept asking myself questions of this kind.

This inspiration continued for several months, as if I was being commissioned to write by a reality bigger than myself, a time during which I was consumed by my experience. It exhausted me. I would sit for hours writing down and revising one verse after the other after the next, unable to temper my creativity or put my pen down. In this simply but deeply complex process, I slowly realized the magnitude of this creative energy that I had begun to channel. It was trying so desperately to come alive in my conscious side.

Carl Jung once said, "Man does not possess creative powers, he is possessed by them."

A balance was being restored in my psyche, I noticed with continued reflection. More importantly though, what had begun was a spiritual healing that I so desperately needed.

I have been practicing Centering Prayer and meditation for several years, but hardly felt any deeply acknowledged changes in my emotional state or behavior. Looking back, I realize that the healing had begun long before what delicately took place at the river. Now, it only reached the level of fever, in what was for me a life transforming experience. Of course, the whole experience could be dismissed as some electrical brain activity with no significance, except that when you live through such an inspiration perhaps, more accurately it lives through you, there is an undeniable presence that tugs you out of this dream state or illusion, into a condition in which there is nothing to prove or defend. Essentially, nothing could take away this powerful experience from you.

I often struggled with the enigmatic and paradoxical nature of Jesus's parables and sayings. Reading the gospels through the lens of Jungian psychology opened my eyes. Only then it became clear to me that Jesus was not talking exclusively about the material or worldly aspects of our lives, but most importantly, Jesus was centered on the inner life or the unconscious mind.

Spirituality and Jungian psychology are deeply interrelated, so much so, that it's impossible to draw a bold line between the two deceptively indistinct fields. For what good is spirituality if it doesn't lead to a deeper knowledge of ourselves? That we might understand the nature of those energies and motives born as part of us, living in us and acting on us constantly, is the answer.

Having actively participated in my opportunity to live through it, this experience helped me to understand my hidden motives at a much more intricate level, making sense of my struggles, accepting myself as I am, enhancing my ability to rest in a state of unknowing and bestowing upon me an enduring sense of wonder and awe of this mystery that we call life. Now, I am full of gratitude as I never have been before.

Namir Stephan

April 4, 2020

Bloomfield Hills, Michigan

"The day of my spiritual awakening
was the day I saw and knew I saw
all things in God
and God in all things"

Mechthild of Magdeburg

"Who looks outside, dreams;
Who looks inside, awakens."

Carl Jung

"It is in the struggle with our
shadow self, with failure, or with wounding
that we break into
higher levels of consciousness"

Richard Rohr

Acknowledgment:

My thanks go to Ed Markowski for introducing me to this particular style of poetry, Cherita, and for encouraging me to publish my work.

My thanks also go to Catrina Stephan for editing the preface to the book.

Contents

1- Restless

Dis-ease in the air

I stumble on the wide road after midlife
facing headwind in despair

looking for shortcuts
for life's easy answers
I was no heir

Watered down graffiti

I'm lost in the blues
staring at walls of myths and history

I scramble for clues
something to lean on
I drift on layers of unsolved mystery

Unfulfilled life

Weary in a culture that offers
"stuff" I used to adore

People out hoarding
money power fame
to life there must be more!

In my dreams

Fast moving clouds
I'm inside walls of stained glass

Hail and dark stormy skies
I'm threatened
dis-ease just wouldn't pass

My ego unsettled

Speeding, passing, endless comparing
a roaring engine feels superior

Flat affect, deflated
left behind on the motorway
doesn't take much to feel inferior

What you see of me

My persona, a book cover
my mask

Trying to show the world
who I'm not
hiding is not an easy task

A high speed train

Uninvited thoughts in my head
moving in circles without permission

My attention hijacked on board
I live in survival mode
in any and every condition

When I was four

I had a train
then I knew how to play

It also went in circles in a magical world
stirred my imagination
for hours a day

Restless

Inside my own skin
wish I'd become another

Running, escaping, trading places
trading ... misery
I knew I shouldn't bother

More dreams

Now intense and vivid
a sense of urgency creeping

Anxious I take painkillers
yearning for awakening
while others were sleeping

Standing on a revolving planet

From daydreams I land in nightmares
counting journeys around the sun travelled

Trapped in my mind's logic
spinning my wheels
kept me baffled

Some mystical moments

My mind would freeze
nothing-spectacular wind or gentle breeze

For a brief moment
it's all over
out of words I thought ... Jeez!

Thanks to Amazon

I was deeply drawn
lots of books and theories some my own

From its gravity I couldn't escape
around my neck
hung the philosophers stone

The universe isn't shy

One thin layer at a time
stripping naked ready to pose

Life begins to expose
meaning
twinkling right under my nose

2- Nature and Duality

A groaning womb in pain

Longing solitude giving birth
an ever-evolving narrative

To sniff the meaning of life
prophets and mystics
thought imperative

From the pulsing heart of Earth

Rapids and rivers
blood in our veins flowing

An unwavering outgoing impulse
keeps
this vigorous bang going

A ruthless drive

Striving and bold
in depth and breadth no fence can hold

Passions to build and destroy
fuel our engines
reaching for newness with every threshold

Footprints of a blueprint

Arteries feeding life a bronchial tree
naked branches of a tree

Veins and rivers
drain into
hearts oceans and sea

In dark silent space

Felt everywhere
resilience of a tree root

With no mercy
ice fractures a rock
the two have no dispute

Programmed to dance

Moon orbiting Earth
planets around the sun

By fractal patterns
connected
on divine programs run

Face to face

Opposites with oneness
original and innate

God split living fabric
to experience
creation and relate

Amnesia to the self

Hypnotized
my ego slowly fell asleep

A loud noisy world
sirens and alarm clocks
trauma cuts in the deep

A neural net

Non-duality I try to perceive
with intellect's tool and symbol

I attempt to catch
living water
my hands shake and tremble

The observer effect

A field of preexisting potential
unfolds into world of twos

Things endlessly
split and rejoin
create one with different hues

What goes up must come down

Water running high to low
one moment a river next a fall

A fair lady in flaring red
to his knees
a man will fall

Men seeking the light

Follow clouds and dark smoke
ponder softness of the moon

Take refuge
under the sycamore
in the blazing sun at noon

In pursuit of the truth

Wrote notes high and low
chanted vespers with sacred tunes

Walked bare footed in vigor
on rocky shores
and hot dunes

I lose my balance

I turn for answers here and there
bouncing in zones of opposites a trap

Going aimlessly in circles
inside an maze
without a map

A shattered dream

Life's meaning like flour out of jars
in fields of thorns blown to scatter

Bare footed men asked
to bake and serve
hot bread on a platter

Finding my inner temple

Self-inquiry and reflection
grow in wisdom a boon

From ashes I know I came
to ashes
I go soon

Should I believe or know

If I'm not the body or the mind
I'm not sure what's left of me

But in one form
or the other
Part of the Omega I'll be

She lives forever

My soul throbbing and vibrant
didn't start in a womb

My nature resonates
with the source
she's not ending in a tomb

My unique identity

Is that all I'm worth!
or all will end in demise

In awakening
on the other side
I'm in for a big surprise

True or false

My false self a stumbling stone
I'll eventually surrender

Free hands can almost touch
the true one
humble and tender

I stand like a mystic tree

A creature with conscious perception
we too need to prune

Cuts and bruises
dissolve in oneness
to illusions become immune

3- Being Human And Attraction

A spectrum of feminine to masculine

In each body and psyche
Adam and Eve on a secret date

In a predetermined direction
grow towards one
or the other state

Meeting of yen and yang

Two on one scale
romance for reunion will create

Transformed by passionate love
accelerated
by such heat and rate

The heart field

Sensual hormone Fueled
psychic driven uncontrollable

As night follows the day
meeting and mating
are inevitable

Two cells exchange vows

In a dark sanctuary
a silent wedding to the future projected

Unfold on a screen
for better or for worse
not yet perfected

In the darkness of a womb

From nowhere a flow starts
a restless heartbeat

Till in God our hearts rest
life giving
from head to feet

An evolving creation

Budding from each other
traits and features we inherit

Uniformity
immense diversity
and a brilliant spark of spirit

A steep mountain cliff

A river looks forward to fall
on rocks becoming mist

Endless forms
it takes and rise
only brief moments exist

4- Drama, Inner and Outer

A new book comes alive

The cover opens at conception
blank papers await their pen

Earth spins
turning the pages
born stories are acted out by men

The show is sold out

Opens with light and shadows
"In the beginning" a script invented [1]

In a dark mysterious backstage
behind a curtain
unconscious persons direct it

Beyond all mc^2 = e

Energies on earth
clearly physical and psychic

To survive the journey
I weave a persona
from opposite traits I pick

Blindfolded knights

Endowed with choices and will
blind to our purpose

In the midst of whining noises
perception provides
enough reasons to be nervous

Enemies or allies

I climb a hill of imagination
view armies of untamed forces

Personal and archetypal
on unconscious horizon
riding our horses

Energies born in the background

drive our motives
regardless they'll react

Appear in dreams
befriend them
they make a pack

A slick diplomat

A strong ego to negotiate
weak ones they'll overpower

Take over the driving wheel
dictate the action
and the hour

What happens in Vegas

Walking with blind inner eyes
the world becomes unrealistic

Fed hollow values
starved men
become narcissistic

Who has the final word?

A referee sitting on a fence
conscious in silent space

Vigilant to thoughts and motives
ready to
block or embrace

Threatened in both worlds

A personality with a blind ego
collapsed on its weight

A skeleton
makes it possible
for flesh to walk or stand straight

5- The Split And The Urgency To See

A box full of pearls

Jewels of great value
sought after by the kingdom

To help us enter a narrow gate
merchants
will pay a great sum

Another layer of reality

Hidden qualities and talents
in consciousness come alive

Embodied in life
even in ritual
they'll empower and help us contrive

A secret world of energies

Nor good nor evil
of divine purpose seek attention

Ignored they raise hell
turn up the heat
with good intention

A living wellspring

Pure the water and clean
we lower a bucket to drink

Abandoned it dries out
an empty well
will stink

No justice no peace

Imagine ten pit bulls adopted
only five you revel

Five you lock up
and starve
become your devil

Turned inside out

An enemy I've created
part of my deepest self

Projected onto others
sitting
in my drawer shelf

Motives in myth and fairy tales

Wisdom of centuries
in gods and demons dressed

The unconscious
not a repository
a valuable treasure chest

Power and life force

Not a dumpster
as earlier thought

Riches
in my backyard
I never dug or sought

A child is punished

A wound opens
running into a world of chaos

Blinds our egos
to the purpose
of our drive and Eros[2]

I always felt there's a vacuum inside

Lack of self-awareness
I filled up with worldly stuff

There is always room for two
finding my soul
is more than enough

Wise men said know thyself

Have courage
for a deeper inner view

Delved in uncharted territory
serious conclusions
they drew

The Hadron collider

Particles accelerated and smashed
smaller ones are detected

With every conflict and offence
a personality
cracked and dissected

Excavations reveal

Layers of the underworld
separated by rocks and shale

Exploring the mystery
by walking down
the trail

A force to be reckoned with

The unconscious charged and alive
personality complexes strive

To fulfill their purpose and do
so at higher consciousness
we arrive

It sounds abstract

Vague at most
till you learn with what you're dealing

A slow process
without which
there's no meaningful healing

Climb the mountain

Grow as part of what life offers
in owe to what flows through

Experience will impregnate you
and give birth
to life's meaning in you

Drifting in the unconscious sea

Without a mystical compass
the world becomes an illusion

Till you awaken to the drama
and come to
the same conclusion

---

120 volts from 10000 volts

gods from God
shadows from light

Transform
lead into gold
in the heart of silent night

____

6- psycho-Spiritual Growth

A territorial dispute!

Settle with your adversary
on the way to court

A judge will condemn
with no trial!
whatever you purport

I am the one to awaken

I'm presumed guilty
burden on my shoulders

Jesus claims
only I decide
to make peace and cross the borders

One hundred sheep

One is lost
the rest remain

A shepherd leaves the ninety-nine
to restore wholeness
or become insane

At war with myself

My personality split in two
of which I wasn't aware

I became
my own adversary
who I couldn't view or bear

In my father's house

I became an older brother
self-esteem I wouldn't give up

With my inner brother
I refused to share
a drink from the same cup

The poorest in unconscious slums

Considered unworthy by men
elevated by God and raised

Rich men in hell tormented
at Abraham's face
Lazarus gazed

God never had plan B

In hubris with the shadow
a gulf the ego created and suffers

Christ to hell descended
shining his light
to find the others

An open field of wheat

Good seeds sown
on days with plenty of sunshine

In a shadowy night weeds grew
both remain
till harvest and twine

Coexist with myself

Rainwater they draw
nourished from the same soil

Pulling the weeds
early on
will uproot the wheat and spoil

———

True colors are all colors

Wheat and weeds inside
of good and evil we're made

Pretending we're one or the other
the parables
to the contrary said

———

As inside is outside

What other basis for forgiveness
all excuses will abolish

Forgive the enemy
in both worlds
our goodness will flourish

———

Striving for self worth

Respect, dignity and pride
we crave but we're confused

Riding with
horse blinkers
but from inside they're infused

A sharp attitude

A branch cut off the vine
from mindfulness we veer

Sense perception
filtered
by self inflated mind sphere

A state of presence

Fears rush in
announce your soul dead

You declare she's deeply asleep
take her hand while dreaming
her soul will rise in a leap

Programmed to believe

Who we're not in essence
the form we've been given

A bigger reality is denied
the world and the media lie
choices made by a frantic mind

____

7- Suffering

My deepest fear

Aware for a brief moment
next it's dark and bleak

The journey a free gift
one chance
to peek and speak

Psychic blindness epidemic

Men rushing in their steps
with their pupils widely opened

Towards a cliff out of space
death lurking
at every moment

Time for a BASE jump!

The chute old and defective
plunge into their eminent death

Eyes of their eyes closed
since they took
their first breath

The story ends

Blood dries out
published or not the book will close

Life's pens keep adding
stories
and endlessly compose

Different genres

Ephemeral joys with
various shades of colors

Interwoven with
unspeakable
misery pains and horrors

Seems like unnecessary suffering

Coming from man and nature alike
a meaningful balance is hard to strike

Some are born
with all that life offers
some are told to take a hike

Nothing goes to waste

In a continuum life flows
a teenager will never leave

The grown up who goes back
finds a wounded child
will grieve

If given a choice

I would probe this life
before being created and tested

On a signature of the author
and reminders
I would have insisted

The imago Dei

Hiding in creation
in darkness

Awaits in patience
for the ego
to heal from blindness

I'm an old dim pond

You throw a stone in me
Circles of fresh waves I become

You live in me
carry me outwards
I thirst for the center I come from

8- Original Innocence

Original innocence

Pure energy sparkling with joy
untouched by harsh reality yet

Lives eternity
with a simple toy
no selfish ambitions set

Unconscious oneness

Instincts of survival
psyche fragile to any offense

A child in his heaven
whole
a bundle with no pretense

In discovery mode

Un-programed unconditioned yet
Pure being

Looking with eyes of wonder
sheer experience
in a vast world of splendor

In a Zen state

With amnesia
child-like whole and sound

It's hard to enter the narrow gate
after being conditioned
fed and crowned

Addressing the crowds

Pointing to a little one
"Unless you become like a child" [3]

If too serious He smiled
doors close
while you're in the wild

Little voices with young energies

Pure and creative
spontaneous playful trusting

At the mercy of others
innocence cracks
once we start adjusting

A crown with jewels is shaken

Trust is the first jewel to fall
false fears are born

In every insult and trauma
insecurity grows
as all the others are torn

In sickness and ill health

Paralyzed by fear
like a virus downloaded

Living
in survival mode
equanimity eroded

9- The Illusion

A crowded mind space

A world with sharp edges
we live in an unrefined condition

We become
self-centered and callused
beyond recognition

A moaning train of thoughts

Attention hijacked
the mind won't give back

Dragged along
entangled
kept on a straight track

A world of Maya

Time is an illusion
exists only in the head

By the clock's hands
and on batteries
survives and constantly fed

The Matrix is a documentary

"We're lived by powers we pretend to understand"   [4]
open our mouth and move our hand

Surrender our will
unconscious
we build a house in the sand

Mr. obsessive compulsive

The inner tutor
you never hired

Points to incessant
thoughts and actions
things you never desired

A dream studio

Symbols borrowed from the world
movies in a dark room created

Portrays the drama inside
a forgotten language
long debated

I watch Netflix

No time for my inner beasts
oblivious to their lively nature

Busy holding on
what belongs to Caesar
become a materially rich creature

A cruise ship on cruise control

Opposing energies
fight for the rudder

Chaotic underworld seems to be
asleep at the wheel
fulfill their motives unwittingly

I strive to earn grace

Chasing a mirage with no clue
as if in a speeding race

Eyes on empty trophies
perception altered
at faster and faster pace

On the opposites cross

My side pierced by a spear
I surrender to fears

My true self cries out
wake up
words fall on deaf ears

10- A Distorted Message

2000 years

Conditioned by church teaching
tedious repetition and ritual

A purpose to live lacking
I escape
what has become habitual

Mired in politics and scandals

My beloved church I blame
superficial understanding seems to be the aim

Contemplation long forgotten
God painted
in a smaller frame

The currency of forgiveness

Hedging the bet on salvation
Jesus paid the expense!

For the creator
to trade and profit
just doesn't make sense

Thinking forbidden

A God you please ... out of fear!
guarding his kingdom's gate!

Going along with the herd
you'll surely
swallow the bait

An out-sightful paradox

A relationship based on fear
when we claim "God is love"

Contradict ourselves
heavy burdens
products of mind stuff

He doesn't play dice

God declared his creation good
in poetry billions of years ago

Lives and sustained
in one direction
on a trajectory placed to grow

Hanging on a tree

A crowned naked man
on golden pendants looks keen

Blind egos just couldn't see
purity codes
won't keep you clean

A handful of righteous men

Contaminate our faculties
illusions of pureness

Guilt and burn in hell
occasionally at the stake
when Jesus taught newness

God loves me ... but!

In a reward and punishment system
I was raised and trained

Fear of adventure
in me
was deeply ingrained

I become religious not spiritual

Creativity suppressed
by family church and schools

To grow my soul
without elders
I'm left with no tools

The manger remains empty

It's not all about lighting candles
a tree or hanging a star

But learning to
dig deeper
discover who you really are

In a small fishing boat

Go into the deep
catch the meaning he meant

Fishing in shallow waters
centuries
we spent

Rewind to 327 A.D.

Deep Gospels essence
ignored and resisted

Empowered bishops and priests
on shallow sermons
insisted

In a vineyard I was told

My wineskins rugged and old
get out of this mind of mine

Get new skins
to pour
new wine

Young souls grow in containers

Mature religions with boundaries
cultivates your spirit and pour

When life calls
for the challenge
with free spirit you soar

Dark death of the soul

Plagued by guilt and shame
we're sinners constantly reminded

Without "falling upwards"   [5]
and pain
we remain blinded

11- New Seeing

With closed eyes

All my life I was taught
what to see in being

Open eyes
was all I needed
and a new way of seeing

A walk in nature

Living art evident to me
the unwritten bible

For that I didn't need
a man
with a collar or a title

No nonsense

Jesus filled with spirit
dismissed religious jargon

Missed no chance to heal on a Sabbath
with tax collectors
made a bargain

He spoke the truth

In cities He walked around
it came out on shore and mount

He rarely hangout in temples
so everyone
would hear the sound

After two millennia

The voice echoes
across the valleys and peaks

If he listens carefully
is heard
by the one who seeks

12- The Invitation

A burning flame

A holy woman I once met
shed light on mystical teaching

My heart stirred by her love
not
by Sunday preaching

Her skinny hand

Pointing to my heart
she whispered

Take a leap and dive inside
deep then deeper
you'll find your bride

In marriage

No human will fulfill you
no companion will fit or complete

Healing unconscious energies
inner union
makes you whole and discrete

An open invitation

Everyone is handed a garment
invited to the wedding

Crippled and the least fit
in society's eyes
to the king's banquet heading

A fancy soup kitchen

A spacious kingdom
to the feast all summoned

It's not about wits or intellect
all are welcome
no membership to club or sect

From a singularity

"Everything Belongs" [6]
a heavenly melody, universal songs

Harps trumpets and music
my heart
from eternity longs

Your blind ego will fight back

Set on old paths with momentum
hanging to illusions

A goal seemingly finalized
when stakes
by the mind analyzed

A painful sight

I seek to look with eyes of a brother
at myself as if in a mirror

A mind differently wired
will shock me
and cause some horror

I wipe my lens

To access a deeper place
from my eyes remove the plank

Withdraw my projection
confess to myself
and be frank

The cosmic Christ

A name for all creation
a universal reality

Made visible in the Son of man
the microcosm
who doesn't belong to a clan

Space is not empty

"In Christ all things hold"   [7]
sounds like quantum theology

Shows the lack of
dividing limits
between physics and biology

13- The Kingdom Within

"Be still and know" [8]

The stillness you come from
stop lip service no babble

If not, Jesus said
for the truth
you'll continue to grapple

Like pop-up art

Jesus's parables
out of the book began to shine

Stories of the gospels
now became personal
and mine

A graceful hidden impulse

The yeast irrelevant in itself
a mustard seed so tiny

The kingdom lies
deep within
flimsy not so shiny

Within us and now

There is no science to describe
kingdom stands for dimension

Heaven a spacious place
infinite potential
in creation to ascension

A seed falls to the ground

A well cultivated soil
plenty of sun shine and rain

The false self is abandoned
creativity grows
free of commandment

Drawn by the salt-less sea

With nostalgia to the shore
God's ways not our ways

A ship doomed to sail
"Breathing under water"   [9]
I'm in the belly of a whale

14- Seeking The Light

A mouth can only utter words

Ask, seek and knock
the door shall open

My ego vigorously knocking
all my knuckles
were broken

Is it wishful thinking!

Am I losing my mind?
I often used to wonder

Discouraged
I'm cautioned
this must be a blunder

A heart can pray

In the present moment
emotions of a lifetime appealed

Espouse desire
feeling is born
greets a divine field

Somewhere in time

A gentle hand
opened a keyless door

Thrown backwards
I met a gush
of my trapped emotions in store

An outer physical reality

Out of convenience
we easily grasp and see

Yet the kingdom within
we readily
desert and flee

A chakra in my head

The lamp of the body
the inner eye I read

I misunderstand
short sighted
it's pitch dark instead

Scales fall of the eyes

At first
you penetrate the illusion

You have a vision
the mind fills
with confusion

Rationality comes to an end

A dark night of the soul will follow
with no answers and deprived

The mind space
becomes
hollow

15- The Dark Night

A fire ignited

Dead branches catch it
in my heart

Turning everything to ashes
my big dream
crumbles and crashes

Deep at the bottom

In stillness
confronted by a mirror

Ghostly images
emerge
with utmost horror

From the corner of my eye

Did I see a liar wave!
a thief! I can even cheat

In disbelief
I couldn't be convinced
my whole self to meet

I buy insurance

A hypocrite I thought
for sure I'm not

I already paid
for a big
heavenly lot

I'm disoriented I'm sick

Is this the narrow path? I prayed
indeed, a true self voice said

Go wherever it takes you
the spirit is playful
no absolute terms are laid

The earth not big enough

"Foxes have dens and birds have nests"   10
exactly how I felt

Unlike the son of man
in disbelief
I lamented and knelt

___

My soul tormented

Torn apart
two halves warring with force

Only grace I thought
can help heal
and end their divorce

___

My wonder child

Unable to grow
left a painful scar

Half ego half shadow
my game
was over par

___

Suffering from the shadow's arrow

Helped me realize
the source of sorrow

Few more arrows
will kill my soul
courage I need to borrow

———————————————————————

I feel incomplete

I left the Ninety Nine
looking for the missing

Down thousand steps
to free the wounded one
in shadow prison

———————————————————————

A man approached him

Asked about suffering
the Buddha gave a parable

Don't waste time
questioning
life is short and we're valuable

———————————————————————

The wise Buddha gave advice

You can live without suffering
but it's not the whole story

just the opening
a drama follows
let's see what's happening

Shot by an arrow and in pain
a man looks for the source
Should I remove the arrow first?
a wise man said, but of course!

This theme kept repeating
one day after the other
Everyday a new arrow removed
the next day another

The man discouraged and hurting
decided to approach the source
To a dark forested area
rode on back of a horse

With hesitation he disembarked
hollered ... who is there?
A battered forest man with sores
came out at him to stare

A beam of light made its way
shone over the forest man's face
The resemblance startling
our man shocked froze in place

Is this my twin brother? He thought
is it possible, shooting my arrows at me!
Lost in the shadow of my heart
my brother I couldn't see

He approached him slowly
there was an embrace
Things lightened up
in this sacred unconscious space

As he was about to leave
the forest man held his hand
Let's look for the others he whispered
so your heart would expand

Down via Delarosa

Holding my opposites cross
scourged by flames of fire

Spiraling down to hell
wasn't my selfish ego's
desire

I'll drink this cup

I'll remain here
but I'm tired of wearing a mask

One question that matters now
what is the true me like?
I ask

16- Exposing The Fear

A little flower

Opens before her time
a hummingbird noticed

Earth had spun to a fresh spring
joy and warmth long awaited
new tidings with it to bring

Fears upon fears

Piled up like hills of ice
melt to reveal a spacious charming paradise

Bigger than
our failures and successes
and a worldly promise full of lies

Tracing the source of fear

Anger
in the face of others

Transferred to my heart field
sense of security
smothers

Emotions bubble up

We turn pale
a world perceived as lacking

There's abundance beneath the surface
untapped treasure
vast and whacking

Skirmishes in the dark

Fear attempts a comeback
for peace I had to hanker

A truce
in the waters
where I dropped the anchor

Revival of inner persons

New and old
with fear released

Converse
in harmony untold
concerns were eased

———————————————————————————

Align yourself

Your thoughts
the universe will dance

All you need
to do
put out your hands

———————————————————————————

A dream-like state

The face of love ethereal
a hidden presence I couldn't dismiss

Soft vespers in my ears
angel lips
touch my cheek with a kiss

———————————————————————————

Realization expanding

Consciousness will stretch
your heart's cords

Playing jazz
with passion
and genres of all sorts

Empty fishing nets

Now you throw left and right
schools of fish are caught despite

Despite anxious emptiness a respite
unrealized abundance
not yet in sight

A blind ego is threatened

In dark waters of the unconscious
grandeur about to sink

Crises mode a panic attack
alarms flash
and ring

An ego drowning

A near death experience
inner eye opens

A tunnel of light
truth shines
regains back its sight

A revived ego stands

Now a decorated knight
lays down his sword

At the feet of his queen
persona sacrificed
with a great reward

A hostage is released

From unconscious tyranny
now true-self serving

Complex free
purified from
the world's debris

Our fears crippling

Stuck in our ways
taxing love with a toll

Channels we refuse to become
willingly
play our role

———————————————————————————

I feel vulnerable

Ignorant to who I am
I hide in a bunker

To reprogram my mind
shame and guilt
I had to conquer

———————————————————————————

A young dragon grows inside

Fed by flames of illusions
I'm paralyzed outside

A bigger dragon
takes over
every time I hide

———————————————————————————

A seesaw in my backyard

A mind caught in extremes
balance will not attain

Polarized opinions
doubts and mistrust
our energies drain

A chain reaction

Ignorant to our makeup
the nature of our pains

Early trauma
recurrent threats
the life force restrains

17- Inner Work

Thundering war drums

A battle only you can fight
zeal for living regain

As if your life depends on it
slay the dragon
or be slain

In a moonless night

A cloud of unknowing
faces frantic and pale

I reach out to help
in my hand I feel
the pain of a nail

Why all this pain

I go insane
to stretch my unconscious open!

Emotions serve
a reminder
something inside is broken

———————————————————————————

Reflect on yourself

Your psychic background
creativity will set you free

"My teaching easy and burden light " [11]
most nod yep
egos disagree

———————————————————————————

The bridegroom is late

Five wise virgins got extra oil
they refuse to lend

Five foolish virgins
ran out of oil
towards the very end

———————————————————————————

Inner homework

You're required to do
it's not served on a plate

No one will awaken
your ego
if you mindlessly await

Rest in mindfulness

Reflect with focused awareness
practiced every single day

Will put you in a spot
show you
where to pray

Closer to the center

"Pray in your inner room and close the door" [12]
inside brick walls you'll never glimpse your core

In the desert forty days He spent
covered by skies
his temple the outdoor

Go through your passions

Truth will pull you down to hell
before it sets you free

At the end of the tunnel
there's light
if you have eyes to see

An expanding circle

Know yourself good and evil
the soul will cheer in delight

You'll be rewarded
with inner friends
almost all day and night

As inside is outside

Love your enemies inside
and extend a hand

Your outer friends circle
will grow
and expand

18- Loneliness

From a distance

Love your family and friends
but hate their ways, too unreasonable!

To enter the kingdom
with sleeping crowds
in Jesus' mind is inconceivable

Learn by subtraction

Images we create
our will rigid and stern

To love with
heart, soul and mind
teach the latter to unlearn

A sweeping collective mind

Nothing is risk free
from the herd depart

Knowing
all is connected
nothing can fall apart

Invest your silver coin

Talents entrusted to create
it is the master's will

Don't run away
from experience
try double your skill

The second half of life is the last

The first is all about discovery
ways of life and growing

Ultimately should lead to
not only knowledge
but deeper knowing

With sentimentality

and attachment
you wrestle

Don't forget
to ask
at who's service is this castle?   [13]

Life will give an unwavering answer

if you're willing to start
so listen

Open the ears of your ears
to the vibration
of your heart

Lifted up by the wind

Hidden high in a cloud
he knows there's a kite

A child feels the pull
even when it's
out of sight

Anxiety levels rise

A smoke detector flashes
we try to numb the fear

Don't run for the exit
it's a message
so dear

An alien alphabet

Almost theatrical
play different roles for a change

Align yourself with
the universe
widen your imagination's range

Saints or not

"In falling and in rising we're held in love"
in a mystical vision "both are from above"   [14]

"In all disorder a secret order"   [15]
nothing left to chance
part of a plan sort of

A ritual of initiation

Love will shake you
push you off the cliff

Dive
instead of falling
never become stiff

Things fall apart

It so appears
emotions high tide a big fear wave

It's all about
loss and renewal
what we destroy life will save

"No feeling is final" [16]

The great poet said
"Just keep going" never turn your head

Keep a slow pace
facing head wind
your wings will spread

The gravity of love

To the plow set your hands
no looking back

To enter the kingdom within
persevere
stay on track

19- A Bigger Reality

I'm not in control I never was

Life happens to me
In me through me and "despite of me"[17]

With lots of things I don't agree
God's will be done
I guarantee

Running out of time

Why not participate
in this grand plan

Not as planet owners
but a brotherhood
of man

In a wooded valley

All trees with one voice
to earth we're firmly connected

Just cause we move and hop
uprooted minds
reject it

It makes cosmic sense

Animated earth we are
our substance from holy stars

Forged with heat and pressure
to flesh blood
and a repertoire

Standing tall

Tree branches
for heights are suited

No tree grows tall
if not in earth
deeply rooted

A gentle breeze

Trembling tree leaves
words and rhyme from earth

A flower grows wings with colors
to a butterfly
gives shape and birth

I see dangling grapes

Long lines of vine
having drawn the colors of earth

Turn into wine
and in our heads
to fantasy will give birth

Illusions of separation

Bound to earth our mother
invisible umbilical cords

Air, water
Unconditional love
Not dividing swords

Back to source

Waters long for the center
to gravity will surrender

Rivers flow with no resistance
into a vast ocean
of splendor

Violence and fragility

Inherit in matter
forms created only at the end shatter

Mightier breaks the weak
the defenseless
to the slaughter

From far on a foggy day

I see a shape and form
but a fountain is just flow

So are we flowing matter
unnoticed
just cause it's slow

Life in action

Elements taken in and expelled
constantly sustain

Our living forms
which seemingly
unchanged remain

What you see of me

A snapshot in time
constant flow no matter

I look the same
just replaced
totally different matter

The flow is full of joy

Fountains can also feel pain
in the words of Marley

Some people
get wet
some feel the rain [18]

Call it love call it spirit

Moving in a flow
manifested and expressed

It takes inner eyes to stare
in darkness
yet be existentially impressed

To evolve is to change

You can't step in
the same river twice

Thinking that we're ever lasting
end up paying
a hefty price

We're perishable

In a life span
nothing will forever grow

We might never know
but will poetry die
when humans go?

The master said

"The heavens and earth shall pass away
and my words will not"   [19]

We are God's word and poetry
with whom
He tied the knot

To be present

At fireworks
or gray days with dull rate and rhythm

Life's colors
created to marvel
through our conscious prism

What doesn't change is real

Out of space and time
a bright uncreated spark centered

In experience
love takes shape
when this mysterious world is entered

Bethlehem a town

A spot on a blue globe
children are born in this earthly stable

And a million stars
will shine above
if the star of Bethlehem is not able

A satellite in orbit

Images of earth taken
a canyon is grand

The whole planet
to be marveled upon
not just the holy land

Filled to the brim

Water in your cup
from every cloud and stream

Where each droplet
came from
you can only ... dream!

An abiding baptism

Not once in a lifetime
through out life rehearsed

In the water pools of earth
each cell filled
and immersed

On the road to Damascus

The Apostle's mystical vision was saying
"In him we live, move and have our being" [20]

In us He lives and knows His loving being
all we need is participate
it's not about obeying

Greek islands or Acropolis

Unreserved give yourself to experience
live it well visceral and shell

In the words of Zorba
"If you kiss a woman
then kiss her well" [21]

An outdated curriculum

Why weren't we taught this in church I ask?
did Schrodinger have to take up the task!

Scientism and fundamentalists
repel each other
will science and non-duality blend in a flask?

Christ a word for everything

"In Him all things hold"   [22]
sounds like a physical concept to me

Habitat of spirit
A matrix
where we exist and be

Science catching up

Achievements broad and wide
yet lags spirituality in depth and height

The search for a smaller particle
has no end
created by thought and sight

Life provides

When blood is dark
a new breath is what it needs

Wind carry pollen
fresh waters
invigorate seeds

Nature waiting for us

Where did the rainbow fall?
before the eye could see?

Who heard
the birds sing
before human ear would be?

Then I came

A little child I once was
with eyes and ears was born

A story to be remembered
like that of the oak tree
told by an acorn

The earth gives

The earth takes back
stories it gave

The one consciousness
flows like
a living tapestry wave

An urge to manifest

Be it a painting poem or a tune
art is created and perfected

To show us the source
a mirror
our essence reflected

Pay back your loan

Not even to our bodies we're entitled
every atom in every cell is recycled

A spiritual face we're promised
something
that'll never to be rivaled

Under layers of rocks

Fossil of birds that once flew
beyond amazing what matter can do

How life evolved is a big question
either way we're in
Divine milieu

Nothing goes to waste

As if life feeds on itself
reshaping every time renews

A reality we don't accept
cause our egos
will bruise

Life goes back and forth

A soul needs the world
the world needs a soul

Our actions now have meaning
coming from
some place whole

A wild ride to end

Don't fear death
it's only change of form

When the men panicked
He surely
calmed the storm

The men were still shaken

Yet destined for wholeness
they awaken

Their blind ego's
attitude
to be forsaken

Self-realization

A reality perceived
new eyes of compassion

The logic of ego battles
for me became
old fashion

A tower reaching heavens

Crippled men attempt to climb
to see what's true

A grounded observer
in stillness
enjoys a bird's eye view

20- Healing

If you're thinking of surrender

A skill that flourished and grew
from a talent you were given

Not a weak ego
give up a strong one
for none but all you're forgiven

360-degree view

Wide lens in focused awareness
a vision with inner reform

The ego grows stronger
to stand up
and weather the storm

The fall of narcissism

The ego is released
awakens to the "I"

rises up to see
 it's just the eyelid
not the eye

Live in your body

In stillness breathe in healing
release it breathe out fear

From paranoia turn away
opens
a new frontier

From Paranoia to Metanoia

Get out of your mind
hear me out

If you can do that
in an excited crowd
I certainly doubt

Don't cling to it

Give up your old life
"all healing is release of fear"   [23]

Shed your old skin
and for that
shed no tear

Frightening experiences

Undress them from
fear cloaks they wore

Exposed emotions
is wisdom
that never feels sore

Coming from my true self

Just as the light and heat
from the sun glow

"I want yes and no
to be
MY yes and MY no"[24]

We see the world as we are

As inside so outside
peace inside no fists no blood

As above so below
sitting in stillness
no drought or flood

____

Walk the narrow path

In the kingdom invest
you'll be surprised by joy

Love energy
will manifest
if you unlearn to destroy

____

Prayer of the heart

Ask from a place of abundance
cause nothing is lacking

Prayer is the feeling
thank
before asking

____

Be surrounded by your answer　　25

As if it already happened
just like He fed the crowds

Fish and bread
full baskets
in His mind had no doubts

Edited original teaching

Relearning how to pray
the soul is not starved

From what is
one big stone
infinite possibilities are carved

Nobody is cast out

With gratitude in no time
with all things we're entangled

In heaven "everything belongs"　　26
Even matters
We mishandled

Absent minded skipper

Take back your attention
sail in waters of experience

Don't let the mind steer
out of laziness
or convenience

Participation in love

God to experience in us
sought co-creators not beggars

Connect with the spirit
partner
in all measures

Free will meets potential

In the present moment
we create experiences not ours

To grab and pretend
we're owners
we build egoic towers

My attention untethered

I stay free from attachment
needs to what's essential

A walk in nature
I realize
my God given potential

Privileged to flourish

After a harsh winter a spring
awakens the wild in a tree

And a flower
with five petals you see
wouldn't open just two or three

Inside a Mandala space

Once in a state of wholeness
there's nothing to defend

Symbolized by a circle
the beginning
is where you end

Hearts longing

Eternal oneness
with Whom is glorified in our thisness   27

God's love
for diversity
Put on the mind of Christ's and brilliance

God's suffering

Creation groaning in labor pain
going through the journey isn't in vain

To look and not see
hear and not listen
victory over death sounds almost insane

All will be revealed

A temple is shaken
a veil torn from top to bottom

Creation celebrates
with joy
what it couldn't fathom

21- The Lie

We're ripped off

Unfair unjust world
rich and poor, black and white

The herd looks gray
in the polarized eyes
of left and right

---

we live at the bottom of a triangle

Recognize our dualistic nature
drag and put us under

For thousands of years
different versions
of divide and conquer

"Do not be afraid"   [28]

Have compassion
for Him prominent themes

Powers that be twisted
to "fear of God"
enslaved the freedom dream

____

Follow me

then gave his life
followers lived in conditions dire

Evil crept slowly
garbage piled up
smells unlike church but empire

____

Projecting violence

A stormy mind with thunder
God chased out in exile

In His tranquil ocean of stillness
storm raindrops
reconcile

____

A childish ego

A blind king and tyrant
controlled by his court

Separated from
the self
the kingdom is bought and sold

Perfiction

In realms of past and future
all things are blemished

Only in the present moment
no-thing
is cherished

Too big to grasp

With Him in one body
sounds a bit odd

But be assured
we're
"hidden with Christ in God" [29]

A portrait of Christ

Infinite potential we're created unique
individuals only one of each

God with us
morphing a reality
out of intricate minds reach

22- The Dance

My soul starved

I remain unfulfilled
bigger barns seem to be the goal

For what does a man profit
to gain all
and lose his soul

Under a balcony I propose

Oh my soul my Eros where should I go
to ask for your hand in marriage

I sold all and I bought
two rings red flowers
white horses and a carriage

A perfect match

We've waited for each other
me and you since our birth

Take me in this carriage
to the new heaven
and the new earth

A circle folk dance

Three vessels holding hands
dancing with one intention

Pouring each others love
flowing
in one direction

Join us

There are more spots
they added and a chance

For we're all from eternity
invited
to this divine dance

Try relax

Even if you try
no mind will comprehend no thesis

Close your eyes in stillness
imagine
a heavenly perichoresis   [30]

Limited mind space

Imagine filling a basket
with constellations of stars

Out there is the ocean
try
pouring in few jars

Tough cosmic questions

After a lifetime in this realm
all answers defy

Francis of Assisi
prayed
"who are you, oh God, and who am I"   [31]

A skeptic in the background

Gratitude for what!
I used to wonder

Mysteries came the answer
are not understood
in awe stand under

A hidden treasure

Wherever that is
there will your heart be

There is an urgent call
to remove
the mask and see

The mustard seed has grown

A burning bush tree
death my soul will not dread

The yeast has done the job
not with bread alone
all are fed

A nest of doubts

I get a tweet
you're hypocrite or mystic

I am both no doubts
holding them
I became artistic

A swinging pendulum

Between doubt and belief the mind will go
"I don't need to believe I know"   [32]

Three remain
faith hope and love
and a deeper knowing God will bestow

I'm born I arrive unaware

Welcome to trauma the world declares
wounded I awaken to heal

He lives in me
I learn to love
going home is no big deal

Stay alert

If you hear the humming
don't look up there for a second coming

With a new tune
and a new song
our hearts for him are drumming

Ends meet beginnings

The alpha and omega have shone
in our hearts Christ is born

I know where I came from
where I'm going
in our hearts the conscious Christ is born [33]

(Footnotes)

[1] - Genesis 1

[2] - Eros, in Jungian psychology, is the drive for love and relationship, not necessarily sexual.

[3] - Matthew 18:3

[4] - W. H. Auden "in memory of Ernest Toller"

[5] - Richard Rohr "Falling Upwards"

[6] - Richard Rohr "Everything Belongs"

[7] - Colossians 1:17

[8] - Psalm 46;10

[9] - Richard Rohr "Breathing Under Water"

[10] - Luke 9:58

[11] - Matthew 11:28-30

[12] - Matthew 6:6

[13] - The Fisher King Myth

[14] - Julian of Norwich "Revelations of Divine Love"

[15] - C. G. Jung, on the archetypal figure of the Anima

[16] - Rainer Maria Rilke "Go the limits of your longing".

[17] - Richard Rohr

[18] - Bob Marley

[19] - Matthew 24:35

[20] - Acts 17:28

[21] - Nikos Kazantzakis "Zorba The Greek"

[22] - Colossians 1:17

[23] - "The course in miracles"

[24] - Carl Jung

[25] Neil Douglas Klotz "Prayers of the Cosmos"

[26] - Richard Rohr "Everything Belongs"

27 - John Dunn Scotus used the word "Thisness" to mean uniqueness

28- John 14:27

29 - Colossians 3:3-4

30 - Richard Rohr, "The Divine Dance". Perichoresis is a circle dance

31 - Francis of Assisi

32 - C.G. Jung, "Face To Face" BBC Interview.

33 - Christ is a word for all creation. In this context one can substitute with Buddha, Krishna, Tao, Universe, the one consciousness etc.